a note to parents

Little Owl Fun-time Readers are a delightful series of rhymes which have been specially written to be enjoyed by younger children.

Read the rhymes out loud to your child at first, so that he or she can learn the rhythm of the words. Perhaps later you could encourage your child to read them for him or herself or maybe even to memorize some of the shorter rhymes.

The Silliest Man and other stories

poems by Clive Hopwood and Jeff Stone

illustrated by Heather Clarke,
Edgar Hodges and Paul Crompton

Copyright © 1989 by World International Publishing Limited.
All rights reserved.
Published in Great Britain by World International Publishing Limited,
An Egmont Company, Egmont House, P.O. Box 111, Great Ducie Street, Manchester M60 3BL.
Printed in D.D.R. ISBN 7235 5550 8
1st Reprint

The Silliest Man

The silliest man that I know
planted eggs in the hope that they'd grow.
But he had no luck
so he dug them up
and sold them at 5p a go.
The silliest man that I've met
decided to go to a vet.
So he took his dad
who was feeling quite sad
that his son thought that he was a pet.

The silliest man you could meet
thought that he had to polish his feet.
He greeted the news
that most people wore shoes
with a howl that I couldn't repeat.
The silliest man you could see
built his kitchen high up in a tree.
He often got stuck
since he had to climb up
every time that he wanted some tea.

The Lady From the Library

When I go to the library
to choose myself a book,
the lady there is very nice,
she likes to help me look.

She takes me where the best books are,
she shows me two or three.
The lady from the library
is very kind to me.

The Fire Brigade

If there's a fire I'm always there
to put the fire out.
I point my hose and turn it on
and spray it all about.

I climb my ladder to the top,
I come to people's aid.
If there's a fire, then don't delay –
yes, call the fire brigade!

Our Village

I like our little village green,
I sit upon the seat
and watch the different people
as they pass along the street.
There's Mrs Pinn, she's tall and thin,
she runs the village shop,
and Mr Ben – he's late again! –
and there goes Mrs Mop.

There's the postman on his rounds,
he often stops to chat
with Mrs Cole, a jolly soul,
who's small and round and fat.
And Mr Top – but he can't stop,
he's always in a hurry –
look, there's his boss, who's very cross,
bad tempered Mr Murray.

The village grocer gives a smile,
he's always full of fun.
He sells sweets and other treats,
and talks to everyone.
I like to sit just for a bit
to see who I can see,
and when I call to one and all
they stop to speak to me.

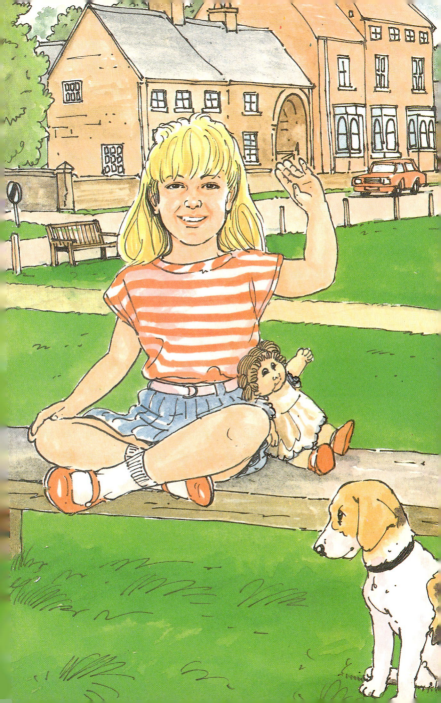

Our Teacher

Our teacher teaches at the school,
she knows her 1,2,3.
We take our turns to show we've learned
to say our A,B,C.

There's no one like our teacher,
she knows all the rules,
but if she's so clever
why does she come to school?

The Postman

One letter, two letters
dropping on the mat,
and if there is a parcel
then the door goes rat-a-tat.

One letter, two letters
coming through the door.
The postman brings our post each day –
I wonder who it's for?

Hubble and Bubble

Hubble and Bubble came from space,
and the first thing they saw was a kettle.
Not being wise, it was quite a surprise
that an Earthman was made out of metal.
Then out of the sky, with no sound at all,
came a man in a green balloon.
Jumping right out with a terrible shout,
he asked if they came from the moon.

The kettle belonged to the Earthman,
and he asked them to stay for some tea.
To have a quick swim they both jumped in
to a river that flowed to the sea.
Deep deep down a crocodile lived,
with a great big smile on his face.
He had been known to eat fully grown
creatures that came down from space.

Hubble and Bubble swam for the bank and
just when they thought they were beaten,
the crocodile spoke, with a horrible croak,
"You're lucky, I've already eaten."
Then it was time to wave goodbye
to the man in the green balloon.
From up in the clouds, they shouted aloud,
"We'll come back to see you quite soon."